The Psychology of Success

Developing a Strong Personality for Success with Emotional Intelligence, Empathy, Body Language and NLP.

DANIEL ROBINSON

© **Copyright 2021 by DANIEL ROBINSON - All rights reserved.**

The following Book is reproduced below with the goal of providing information that is as accurate and reliable as possible. Regardless, the purchase of this book may be viewed as an agreement that both the publisher and author of this book are in no way responsible for the topics discussed within and that any recommendation or suggestion made here is for entertainment purposes only based on their own experience and studies gained over many years. Professionals should be consulted, if necessary, before taking any action advocated here.

This is a legally binding declaration that is considered both valid and fair by both the Committee of Publishers Association and the American Bar Association and should be considered as legally binding within the United States.
The reproduction, transmission, and duplication of any of the content found herein, including any specific or extended information, will be done as an illegal act regardless of the end form the information ultimately takes. This includes copied versions of the work, both physical, digital and audio unless express consent of the Publisher is provided beforehand. Any additional rights reserved.

Furthermore, the information that can be found within the pages described forthwith shall be considered both accurate and truthful when it comes to the recounting of facts. As such, any use, correct or incorrect, of the provided information will render the Publisher free of responsibility as to the actions taken outside of their direct purview. Regardless, there are zero scenarios where the original author or the Publisher can be deemed liable in any fashion for any damages or hardships that may result from any of the information discussed herein.

Additionally, the information in the following pages is intended only for informational purposes and should thus be thought of as universal. As befitting its nature, it is presented without assurance regarding its prolonged validity or interim quality. Trademarks that are mentioned are done without written consent and can in no way be considered an endorsement from the trademark holder.

This content is provided with the sole purpose of providing relevant information on a specific topic for which every reasonable effort has been made to ensure that it is both accurate and reasonable. Nevertheless, by purchasing this content, you consent to the fact that the author, as well as the publisher, are in no way experts on the topics contained herein, regardless of any claims as such that may be made within. As such, any suggestions or recommendations that are made within are done so purely for entertainment value. It is recommended that you always consult a professional prior to undertaking any of the advice or techniques discussed within.

TABLE OF CONTENTS

INTRODUCTION — 7

CHAPTER 1: THE PSYCHOLOGY — 9

The Biological Perspective — 14
The Psychodynamic Perspective — 16
The Behavioral Perspective — 18
The Cognitive Perspective — 20
The Humanistic Perspective — 21

CHAPTER 2: WHAT IS PERSONALITY? — 24

Why Personality Matters — 28
The MBTI Personality Types — 34

CHAPTER 3: THE PSYCHOLOGY OF SUCCESS — 40

Making Your Own Definition of Success — 41
Psychology of Success and Emotional Intelligence — 43
Building Emotional Intelligence — 45

CHAPTER 4: BODY LANGUAGE FOR SUCCESS — 54

How to Control Your Body Language — 54

Confident Body Language _____ 55
Develop open body language _____ 57

CHAPTER 5 USING PSYCHOLOGY TO FIGHT PROCRASTINATION _____ 60

The Problem with Procrastination _____ 61
Why People Procrastinate _____ 63
Defeating Procrastination with Psychology _____ 66

CHAPTER 6: NEURO-LINGUISTIC PROGRAMMING FOR A SUCCESSFUL LIFE _____ 75

La storia della PNL _____ 76
Conoscere il tuo risultato _____ 79

CHAPTER 7: THE IMPORTANCE OF EMPATHY FOR ACHIEVING SUCCESS _____ 89

What is Empathy? _____ 90
Empathy to Increase Self-Awareness _____ 92
Empathy to Build Self-Esteem _____ 94

CONCLUSION _____ 98

Introduction

Congratulations on purchasing **The Psychology of Success**, and thank you for doing so.
If you have ever felt like no matter how hard you have tried in life there always seems to be something going wrong, you are not alone.

In this book you will be guided to the achievement of your goals. You will then be guided through distinct concepts: How psychology impacts your chances at success, and how it can ward off procrastination; understanding the various personality types to recognize yourself in one; how to have open body language and how to use empathy to increase your self-esteem; you will understand how to improve your communication and NLP skills in ways that are favorable to living a happy and successful life. When you understand these concepts, you can then begin to take action.

As you read through this book, it is with the utmost hope that you will find it useful, informative and provide you with advice that you can follow and use to succeed.
There are plenty of books on this subject on the market, thanks again for choosing this one! Every effort was made to ensure it is full of as much useful information as possible; please enjoy it!

Chapter 1: The Psychology

Psychology is the scientific study of the mind and behavior. However, there is so much to the mind and behavior; think of all of the fields within psychology that exist. There are fields dedicated to understanding normal human development, seeing how children grow and learn. Other fields look at abnormal psychology and take a look at how it matters and how to treat it.

Some people study how to learn, while others look at how drugs and other substances may impact the body and mind. At the end of the day, psychology covers anything to do with the mind, both mentally and physically.

Psychology achieves this by having four main goals: To describe, explain, predict, and change the way that people think and act. We will go over each of these goals in a moment, but what is critical to understand here is that these goals drive psychology forward. They make it clear that we act in certain manners for certain reasons and see, to figure it out in order to make any changes if necessary.

Describe

The first goal is to describe behaviors and thought processes. This is critical if you want to be able to understand general rules that are typically exhibited in behavior. For example, if you want to be able to tell how someone is going to behave, you would look at several instances that show exactly how they are going to behave. We observe infants playing to figure out that at some point, something changes and they no longer think that something ceases to exist when it is out of sight. We watch how children interact with each other without guidance to identify when altruistic behavior starts to develop.

Describing and observing create a critical first step precisely because they are responsible for developing a base understanding of standard behavior. In being able to analyze, you must figure out a base norm in order to figure out where the deviations from the norm are.

Explain

After being able to describe the processes of other people, explaining is the second goal. Upon being able to describe what occurs, such as watching the infants seem to come to the realization that, even when mom and dad are out of sight, they still exist, the law can start to be assembled. They can start to figure out *why* this happens. This is what happens during the second goal of psychology—explaining.

Usually, this goal involves understanding what happened—it looks at the description of what has happened in the describe stage and then begins to come up with several theories that may or may not support it. These theories are meant to come up with whatever the explanation is for that particular behavior.
Effectively, the psychologists will try to figure out the most reasonable explanation for why someone does something and then tries to test it.

Predict

As the empirical research yields potential explanations for the behavior being studied, psychology then moves toward prediction as the primary goal. During this stage, the explanations created in the previous step are taken and tested.

If they fail to meet expectations, they are removed from the list, and they will try to come up with something else.

For example, assume that you have been watching your child seem utterly baffled when you disappear and reappear playing peekaboo. You can then assume that your child thinks that you are gone when you disappear. You then predict that your child will react with the same sense of bafflement when you take that ball that he was playing with and cover it up with a blanket because the child will be looking for his ball. You test this out, and sure enough, your explanation was correct.

Change

Finally, once you have been able to describe, explain, and predict the behaviors, you can then begin to understand how to influence change in other people. You may look to help control a negative behavior, such as someone who suffers from anxiety learning to cope with those feelings. You may make it a point to look at someone who has obsessive-compulsive disorder, figure out their triggers, and then figure out how best to help them change that behavior.

Effectively, change allows for behaviors to be modified in order for people to develop healthy coping mechanisms, even when they are faced with difficult situations, disorders, or struggles that make otherwise normal functioning difficult. You can learn how to overcome phobias once you can understand and predict the cause, or you can learn to fix issues with emotional regulation. You can challenge depression. You can correct negative thoughts. You can effectively begin treating the other person's mind when you know how the mind is implicated.

The study of psychology can largely be broken down into five distinct perspectives—each wishes to focus on an entirely different part of the mind. These different perspectives are the biological perspective, the psychodynamic perspective, the behavioral perspective, the cognitive perspective, and the humanistic perspective. Effectively, someone who looks at an issue such as depression from the biological perspective is going to be focused on the biology behind the depression being studied—it will look at neurotransmitters and areas of the brain that are responsible for the feelings. However, someone in the behavioral perspective may be looking for the way that the external world is directly responsible for influencing those feelings of depression.

We will take a look at all five of these perspectives to get a solid working idea of all aspects of what is happening within the mind. While having one specific focus can be incredibly useful, it takes all five to put together a proper, complete view of what is happening.

The Biological Perspective

As you may have assumed, the biological approach is all about how your body impacts your mind. In particular, it is an attempt to understand the link between the mental states and body of someone else. If you are feeling happy, what is going on in the body? There is a physiological change in response to your feelings, and the biological perspective is incredibly interested in looking into it. Effectively, then, you will be looking into how the brain works.

Within the biological perspective, effectively, you and your consciousness are all the collective sum of your body. Your brain all comes together to work through electrical impulses and chemicals, and those tiny impulses are what create you. In the great debate of nature vs. nurture, this is the nature part. It believes that the biology of the brain and body are what are important in determining the behaviors and thoughts of the other person.

Just like the other perspectives, the biological perspective is entirely interested in understanding people and their behaviors. However, they want to look at other aspects. Genetics come into play, as do physical changes to the brain. They may take a special interest in how genetics influence all sorts of aspects of personality, like depression or anxiety, or how brain damage can lead to several issues in ability or behavior. In particular, biological psychologists will look into identical twins, learning as much as they can about the tendencies of people versus what they actually do.

When you are using the biological perspective, you are likely going to use tools to observe the brain as directly as possible. Scans such as a PET or MRI can allow psychologists to view the brain's physical structure in order to begin to make inferences on the behavioral aspects of the person.

In particular, the biological perspective is a powerful one to take—when you use the biological perspective, you are effectively ensuring that you understand the physiology, and sometimes, that is enough. If you know that someone has suffered from a massive stroke and can see exactly where the damage is, for example, you can begin to predict exactly what parts of their behavior are likely to be impacted. It also means that certain behavioral changes may be approached as a sign of a physical medical issue, such as a brain injury or a tumor.

This is also the perspective that would be responsible for ensuring that medication is effective. When the physiological cause is understood, it becomes far easier to begin identifying how best to medicate the issue. If there are certain parts of the brain that are struggling to create enough of a certain neurotransmitter, for example, then that can be medicated for in order to help the body to then help the mind.

The Psychodynamic Perspective

The psychodynamic approach began with Sigmund Freud's psychoanalysis, but it did grow over time to encompass several other theories as well, such as the theories of Karl Jung, Erik Erikson, and Alfred Adler. Within the psychodynamic theory, it is believed that early childhood events influence almost everything. Effectively, during the early childhood period, you are particularly susceptible to being damaged and therefore internalizing issues within your unconscious mind. These lead to behavioral problems that are the results of the unconscious mind.

In particular, you will see within the psychodynamic perspective; the emphasis is placed on the unconscious mind. Think of the mind like an iceberg—only the tip is visible. You can see the conscious part of the mind or the tip of the iceberg, but the vast majority of it is hidden beneath the surface of the water. Effectively, the unconscious mind houses almost everything. All of your motivational impulses are housed in the unconscious. Your feelings will come from it, your motives will be rooted in it, and your decisions will be based upon it.

The unconscious mind, while incredibly powerful, is also incredibly impressionable. This, then, pushes the focus of human behavior from nature to nurture.

Further, within the psychodynamic perspective, you see three parts of personality that arise: The id, the ego, and the super-ego. Your id refers to the instincts—it is inherited and holds all of your natural personality and behavioral tendencies. Your ego is the part of the mind that is meant to sort of mitigate the demands and desires of the id, which is primarily quite unrealistic, and the world around you. This is the part that makes decisions. Finally, the superego is the series of values and morals that are learned from both society and parents.

The id and super-ego are considered the unconscious mind—they both fight to win the favor of the mind (ego). Effectively, your instinctive tendencies toward sex and aggressive behavior will constantly be trying to get you to act impulsively, while the learned portion is trying to keep you in line in order to guarantee that you will not do something that you should not be. The conflict leads to anxiety, which the ego must cope with somehow. These coping mechanisms become the method through which you behave. Effectively, then, the conscious mind is the slave for the unconscious mind, with the unconscious mind making the decisions and controlling. However, the unconscious mind is also influenced regularly by external features and instances. A trauma can, for example, lead to a change in the unconscious mind, which is then noticeable in the behavior.

The Behavioral Perspective

The behavioral perspective places emphasis on the environment on your behaviors. It asserts that you can effectively be trained to do just about anything if someone is willing to put in the effort to do so. When you believe in the behavioral perspective, you reject the idea of free will—you effectively declare that all behavior is learned through either reinforcements or punishment.

Reinforcements refer to consequences that occur after a behavior that is either positive or negative. Positive refers to the fact that something was put in place, whereas negative refers to the act of something being removed. In this case, positive reinforcement is a pleasant situation that is added to encourage the behavior to continue. A negative reinforcement, then, is a situation being removed, usually an unpleasant one, in response to a behavior in order to encourage it to continue happening in the future.

On the other hand, punishment is the act of something happening to discourage a behavior. It is the opposite of reinforcement in the sense that it is designed to be discouraging while reinforcement is enforcing. Like reinforcement, punishment can be both positive and negative. For example, positive punishment could entail adding extra chores in retaliation for not listening or lying about a situation. On the other hand, negative reinforcement is the act of removing something pleasing in order to deter the behavior in the future. For example, imagine that your teen daughter has not turned in several assignments, and she has her cell phone taken away until she gets them all in. You took away something pleasant, in this case, her cell phone, in order to discourage the behavior of continuing to miss assignments.

Behaviorists believe that the above processes are what cause behavior to continue or discontinue. When you enjoy a situation or get something pleasant in response, you want to encourage doing something. When you realize that you have the same bad response every time you try to do something, you are going to learn not to do that behavior any more out of wanting to avoid the negative stimulus. Effectively, in behaviorism, thoughts do not matter—behaviors do. It does not matter how angry someone is about the consequences or how unfair your child believes losing her cell phone was—all that matters is the end result.

The Cognitive Perspective

Cognitive psychologists, on the other hand, assert that behavior is determined due to expectations. You have a certain thought about a situation and expect it to behave that way. Effectively, then, you make expectations that are informed based upon what you already know and try to make the proper inferences in your behavior. In this instance, you are solving problems and interacting with the world based on the memory of what has happened in the past. You assume that what has happened in the past will happen again in the future, or you make assumptions based on similar events.

This takes humanity away from the idea of being completely devoid of free will and instead as something that is capable of thoughts and feelings again. Of course, this also brings with it far more complication than was present otherwise.

Imagine that you have plans to go out with friends for the night. You assume that the night will be full of fun—you and your friends would leave the kids at home, go to a movie, and then have dinner and a few drinks at your favorite restaurant. You get yourself all dressed up and ready, but when you arrive at the meeting place, you realize that two of your three friends have brought their children with them, which means that movie that you have wanted to see is no longer on the table, nor is having a few drinks with dinner, as there are little eyes there.

In this instance, you are probably quite disappointed. You had certain expectations, only to have them completely overthrown, and that can be incredibly difficult for some people to cope with. However, according to cognitivists, you are not disappointed because of the fact that your friends brought their children along to what was supposed to be a kid-free event—you are annoyed because your own expectations were completely and utterly thrown out the window. The fact that the instance did not line up with your own expectations is why you are annoyed and disappointed. It is that thought process and the disconnect that is the root of the disappointment, not the fact that the other parties did something unexpected.

This is where the idea of other people not being responsible for your own feelings comes from—only your own thoughts can influence your behavior, and no one else is responsible for them. Even if someone else does not live up to your own expectations, it is your own job to figure out how to manage that disappointment.

The Humanistic Perspective

Finally, the humanistic approach to psychology emphasizes that humans are motivated by their own inherent goodness. Effectively, people need to be empowered in order to become the best person that they are able to be. They want to offer support without the guidance, to empower individuals to make their own decisions.

Humanistic psychology approaches the situation in a way that directly rejects those behaviorist and psychodynamic approaches that are believed to be too limiting. Instead, people are believed to be entirely free to make their own decisions, and inherently, they will always strive to be better. Those who use the humanistic approach emphasize the idea that people will actively work toward improvement, seeking to overcome difficult situations in order to attain what is known as self-actualization—satisfaction in life.

Effectively, the driving force behind behaviors is not the brain or the environment, but rather the inherent drive people have to better themselves and their situation. Of course, this comes with its own implications as well—humanistic studies inherently reject scientific methodology. They instead focus on qualitative research, like discussing situations. These are effectively useful for individual studies to understand an individual person without trying to figure out the entirety of humankind's behavior.

Chapter 2: What is Personality?

Personality is, simply put, who you are as a person. When you are talking about personality, you are looking at the differences between how you may think, feel, and behave versus how other people choose to think, feel, and behave. It then takes into consideration how those three categories come together to make you as a whole. In general, you may hear people describe someone else as introverted or extraverted, or that they are bold and unique, or maybe timid. These are all characteristics that come together to create your own personality.

Your personality traits come from several different aspects of life—some are genetic inheritances, others are genetic predispositions that required a certain sort of activation somewhere in life, and others still are simply learned responses to the world around you. Ultimately, when you want to look at your personality or the personality of other people, you will be looking at the Big Five Personality Traits. These can be remembered by the acronym OCEAN:

- **Openness to experience**
- **Conscientiousness**
- **Extraversion vs. introversion**
- **Agreeableness**
- **Neuroticism**

Each of these personality tendencies can help you understand who people are as a whole. Everyone will exhibit some level of each of these five traits—it will simply be a matter of figuring out if someone is entirely agreeable or entirely defiant, for example. When you understand someone's tendencies within these five traits, you start to figure out their personality types.

Openness

This particular trait is crucial to imagination or being able to find insight. When someone happens to be highly open to experiences, they tend to be creative and adventurous. They are typically quite curious and want to learn more about the world around them. They are excited about exploring the world.

However, those who score far lower on their openness to experience the world tend to be far more rigid. They like tradition and schedule and are aversive to change in general. They will resist anything that is unfamiliar and usually dislike when conversations or discussions lean toward theoretical. They want to live in comfort without worrying about what will happen next or how they will need to proceed throughout life.

Conscientiousness

This personality trait is all about how thoughtful someone is as an individual. It takes into consideration how likely someone is to be able to control their impulses or make sure that they are constantly working toward their goals. Those who are largely conscientious are usually the ones who pay meticulous attention to details. They feel the need to plan exactly how things will play out and always consider how other people are likely to feel as a result of their own behaviors and tendencies.

On the other hand, those who are not particularly conscientious are usually very dismissive of structure. Things will happen when they happen and not a moment sooner. They do not mind, and sometimes even prefer, the unpredictability of chaos and are usually not particularly disciplined. They will procrastinate or simply fail when it comes to achieving deadlines or goals.

Extraversion

This particular trait encompasses how one views being able to socialize with others. In particular, those who are extraverted tend to feel like they are energized by other people or engaging in social interaction. They tend to enjoy others and will go out of their way to get out and be social.

Those who are not particularly extraverted are usually referred to as introverts, and introverts are typically quite reserved. They feel like they must expend energy when interacting and engaging with people out in public. Rather than being energized by social activity, they feel drained and often feel the need to retreat and relax. This does not mean that they are necessarily antisocial, but rather that socialization, no matter how enjoyed, is exhausting, and they need to spend the time to recharge after the fact.

Agreeableness

This trait looks at trust, kindness, and other behaviors that would be deemed prosocial. Effectively, they are happily cooperative and are willing to help others. In fact, they are usually quite empathetic and care strongly about how other people feel. They want to make sure that they are helping other people. On the other hand, people who are less agreeable typically care about and empathize less with those around them. They do not care much when they see people suffering and may even tend to manipulate others, having no problems with using other people to get what they want or need. All they care about is how they get what they want.

Neuroticism

The last trait is neuroticism—this looks at the emotional instability and moodiness of an individual. When you are highly neurotic, you are typically quite moody in general, with higher levels of anxiety or irritability. You may be easily upset and struggle to cope with stress when you are facing it. Those who are not neurotic; on the other hand, tend to be far more emotionally stable—they are resilient and relaxed. They are able to cope with stress as it arises without worrying too much about it. They can manage their own emotions and are rarely stuck in feelings of despair.

Why Personality Matters

Personality is crucial because it determines how people in the world interact. If you are neurotic, you are going to have a tendency to sway from emotion to emotion, and if you pair that with someone who is not agreeable, you may find that you are dealing with someone who does not care about prosocial behaviors while also oscillating from mood to mood. When you understand what someone's tendencies are, you are prepared to deal with them.

Beyond just that, however, personality determines how you will interact with the world and how those around you will also respond. When you can understand personality and the personality traits of other people, you can make sure that you can predict the behavioral patterns of other people. You can see how other people will react and in understanding that reaction, you will be able to understand what to expect in your own interactions with someone else. You will also be able to identify body language cues that may be important to know.

Myers-Briggs Type Indicator

Perhaps one of the more well-known personality type indicators out there is the Myers-Briggs Type Indicator (MBTI). This particular personality type indicator looks at four distinct modes of interacting with the world that combine to create 16 distinct personality types that all have their own tendencies and determinants.

This particular personality type indicator works on introspective self-reporting, meaning that people are required to go through the test on their own and answer what they feel is the most accurate. Of course, this also means that it can be flawed sometimes—people can skew the test toward traits that they think they have or they wish they would have, and that can bring up some doubts on whether this is an effective or trustworthy way to analyze personality. Nevertheless, it is still useful to offer some insight into the minds of other people.

The MBTI will look in particular at cognitive learning styles—this means that it is focused on how people interact with the world. It is important to recognize that the comparative pairs of traits are not meant to be seen as polar opposites but rather two ends of one spectrum in which the world is viewed. Some people can exist halfway through one category, balancing out in the middle, and someone who is largely on one end of the spectrum can exhibit traits that exist on the other as well.

Introvert vs. Extravert

The first learning style that is looked at is the introvert versus the extravert. In particular, when you are looking at the MBTI, you are going to see the spelling of "extravert," though it is commonly spelled as extrovert in several other sources. Nevertheless, this particular type looks to see how people learn in regards to social interactions.

People on the extravert end of the spectrum usually learn well by interacting with the world around them. They look to the physical world around them in order to figure out what is happening. They are more likely to require being able to touch and feel things rather than simply contemplating it, and they are happy to process in person.

People on the introvert end of the spectrum, on the other hand, prefer to reflect in peace and quiet. They do not require the physical aspect to learning and do better oftentimes when they are able to internally grapple with a concept. They prefer to process internally as opposed to the extravert's external preference.

Sensing vs. Intuition

The next spectrum that is identified is the spectrum between sensing and intuition. This is where people tend to focus their attention in order to understand the world around them. It determines whether people are interested in the physical versus the abstract.

In particular, those on the sensing end of the spectrum tend to favor the concrete and tangible. They want to see the results and have the evidence in their hands and available to them. There is a major preference toward details and sequences, and they want to focus on what is in front of them rather than abstract or hypotheticals.

The intuition end of the spectrum, on the other hand, involves people that are good at understanding and grappling with the hypothetical and abstract. They do not feel the need to have something in front of them, and would rather contemplate what is happening rather than have to interact physically.

Thinking vs. Feeling

The third spectrum identifies the preferences used during decision making. This particular spectrum seeks to identify whether people are more likely to make a decision based on their emotions or versus looking at things logically and rationally. Both forms of thinking have their own important purposes, and it is ultimately a matter of looking at the preference.

People on the thinking end of the spectrum usually look at cold logic and truth. Feelings have nothing to do with their decisions, and they will always look to make objective decisions based upon the truth and evidence that they have in front of them. They are interested in logic and deduction and will go with the logical decision, no matter how much they may dislike the implications or the feelings that go along with it.

The people on the feeling end, however, tend to emphasize the emotions that go along with their decision. They will look at situations in much more nuanced ways, taking a look at the reason behind why someone did something rather than simply judging it to be black or white.

For example, the thinker may say that the person who was stealing is a criminal who deserves to be prosecuted accordingly, while the feeler may point out that the person stole a loaf of bread to feed his children, and that leniency is in order. They are both looking at the same problem, but the thinker believes that things must be logical and follow the rules, meaning the man is guilty no matter what and deserves the same punishment as the people who have stolen for gain rather than to simply survive, while the feeler cares about the motives.

Judging vs. Perceiving

Finally, the fourth spectrum seeks to identify how people tend to regard complexity in the world. People tend to approach the world in different manners, with some choosing a structured, logical manner, while others prefer to go with the flow.

In particular, those who are on the judging end of the spectrum prefer to have a structure to their approach to the world. They enjoy having protocols in place and a pattern for how they will get through the world around them. This structure is used as their guide and helps them know what to expect.

On the perceiving end, however, people prefer to keep things open. They want to be able to have options that will allow for change if it is needed. While the judging types will try to fit new information into their understanding of the world and its structures, the perceivers are more likely to change without needing any sort of previous structure. They are willing to go with the flow.

The MBTI Personality Types

INTJ: The Architect: These people are imaginative and tend to do well with strategy. They are able to develop plans with ease and prefer to always have plans. They question everything as they observe the world around them.

INTP: The Logician: This personality type is categorized as being skilled at analysis. These people are able to analyze quickly and then use those analyses to ensure that they are able to achieve what they set out to do with the possible success.

ENTJ: The Commander: Those with the ENTJ personality types are typically comfortable in a leadership position. They are willing to take charge and are particularly skilled in structure. They typically are driven by ambition and are optimistic and comfortable in making decisions quickly.

ENTP: The Debater: This personality type is driven by the ability to have conversations and learn. They love to engage with other people, welcome challenge and like to look at the world through logic while inviting others to join them as well.

INFJ: The Advocate: The INFJ is all about helping other people. This person has a kind nature and tends to reflect. They are creative and are willing to look at the world with uniquely idealistic perspectives. Usually, these people are visionaries.

INFP: The Mediator: These people are usually interested in figuring out what the meaning of the world is. They are usually quite sensitive and prefer to spend time at home on their own, allowing their imaginations to run wild. Usually, these people are reserved and interested in pursuing their values.

ENFJ: The Protagonist: The ENFJ is usually driven by principles. They are charismatic and find it easy to relate to others while still maintaining their idealistic values. They are usually quite outspoken.

ENFP: The Campaigner: This personality type focuses on creating the path to the life they wish to live. They are interested in beginning new projects while also seeing the potential that other people possess, encouraging, and fostering it.

ISTJ: The Logistician: Those with this personality type tend to be incredibly organized and driven to work hard. They are attentive and are skilled in managing their social and cultural responsibilities. Usually, these people are interested in thinking deeply to identify clearly what is right. They are usually trustworthy and reserved, but also intimidating to those that they do not know.

ISFJ: The Defender: This personality type is determined to help other people. They are usually quite warm and nurturing while also sensitive. They are usually deemed to be loyal, generous, and considerate.

ESTJ: The Executive: The ESTJ personality type is characterized by being traditional and deeply driven by their desire to follow those values they hold dear. They are usually quite happy to lead other people and asked for help regularly because their advice is typically deemed to be orderly and result-oriented.

ESFJ: The Consul: This personality type is identified as being entirely comfortable being in the limelight. They enjoy social interaction and do everything in their power to be liked. They are usually quite gracious and thoughtful, along with being interested in helping everyone around them.

ISTP: The Virtuoso: These people are driven by their desire to be rational. They observe the world around them and then figure out how best to reply rationally. They are usually incredibly spontaneous, bringing with them enthusiasm with a side of pragmatism.

ISFP: The Adventurer: These people tend to be good at listening and focus on being a good friend. They may struggle with that initial connection to others, but once it is made, they value making sure that they and those around them are at peace.

ESTP: The Entrepreneur: These people are the doers—they are willing to go out and do new things. They enjoy spending their time with other people and do not want to have to be bothered with the details. They are good at solving pragmatic problems and negotiating, but they are also usually deemed to be quite impulsive and unconventional.

ESFP: The Entertainer: This personality type is characterized by the ability to bring energy to any event. They are good at interacting with other people, and those skills make them incredibly beneficial to be around. They are usually quite sympathetic and thoughtful about the world around them.

Chapter 3: The Psychology of Success

Success—everyone wants it. Whether you want a successful relationship, a successful career, or a successful life, you are striving for excellence, and that is okay. When you are striving for this sort of excellence, you are telling yourself that you deserve the best of what you have to offer yourself, and that is showing that you truly care about how you see yourself and what you do with yourself.

This is good—you are showing what you are deserving of. You are showing that you know that you deserve the best and that you are willing to put your best foot forward. However, you may feel like it is difficult to get past that point. What is success? How do you become successful? How can you be sure that you ultimately get the life that you feel that you deserve? This chapter seeks to help you answer these questions—we will come up with a definition of success .then, we will discuss how success exists as a psychology within emotional intelligence—and finally, how to strengthen emotional intelligence in order to ensure that you are as successful as you have set out to become.

When you are successful, one thing is for sure—you are opening up dozens of doors for yourself, and in doing so, you are bound to find one that is perfect for you. You will find one that serves you well and keeps you happy. It is simply a matter of finding happiness and figuring out how best to pursue it.

Making Your Own Definition of Success

Success is one of those things that is incredibly personal. Your own definition of success is likely to vary greatly from the definitions of those around you. This is okay—success is something that is entirely for you, so it is okay for it to be personal and varying based on the individual. You should make sure that the definition of success that you create is one that truly encompasses what you want to achieve.

In particular, there are seven steps to defining your own success—if you can follow these steps, you are likely to find that you can find that success for yourself.

First, you must ask yourself what success looks like to you. Figure out what it is that you want out of life and write it down for yourself. Do you want a life that is defined by being comfortable? Perhaps you want to ensure that you are happy. Maybe it is with a partner, exactly three children, a nice minivan parked in the driveway, and a nice, middle-class home that you own. This is a perfectly okay picture of success—if your dream is to have a family. It may be. Ultimately, however, your picture of success should directly reflect what you want in life.

With that picture of success in mind, it is time to make a plan. This is when you figure out exactly how you will achieve that success that you so deeply desire. This step is critical for ensuring that you are actually able to achieve your success—a plan that is not actually planned out is not likely to pan out either, and that is problematic. Make sure that your plan is as specific as possible as you do make it, as well. With a specific plan in mind, you are far more likely to achieve it than you may actually believe.

At this point, you need to make your goal happen. Do what you must and see what happens as a result. Is the other party happy with you? Do you like the results? Was it everything that you ever wanted? This is a critical point in this skill.

Finally, you must determine whether you were actually successful or not. If you were great! If not, try again in the future. You may need to make some tweaks to what you are doing, but it will be worth it when you finish your work up with ease and find that your success has, in fact, been achieved once and for all. In making sure that you never give up, you promise yourself to remain resilient and steadfast in your attempt to achieve success for yourself.

Psychology of Success and Emotional Intelligence

Remember, if you want to be successful, you want to be emotionally intelligent. This means you want to learn to begin with all of those regulation skills that have been discussed thus far. You want to learn if you can, in fact, successfully pull off those stretch goals that you have been reaching for. If you do succeed, great! If not, remember that it is not the end of the world.

Those who are emotionally intelligent tend to also be quite skilled when it comes to coping with stress and discomfort. Thanks to the fact that they are great at self-regulation, you can usually keep the stress and discomfort at bay. This means that you can actively protect yourself in ways that you did not think were possible at some points in time.

Emotionally intelligent individuals are able to cope with the stress and overwhelming feelings that come along with failure as well—when they do face that fear and discomfort, they tend to figure out how best to cope with it. The emotionally intelligent individual may make it a point, for example, to try again. This sort of resilience is critical to those who are trying to be successful. If you can be successful through making it a point to deal with failure, you are effectively learning through trial and error without ever letting someone else hurt or impact yourself negatively.

When you are faced with failure, you instead decide to learn from it. You figure out a new way to tackle the problem, and much of the time, when you do behave in such a way, you find that you are actually far more likely to get further in life. You figure out how best to take care of yourself, and that brings with it a happiness and feeling of success. Effectively, because you continued to try and were perseverant, you eventually found the solution on your own, and that is worthy of praise itself.

This means, then, if you wish to be more successful in general, you want to figure out how best to go about becoming emotionally intelligent. You want to actively become emotionally intelligent to pursue that definition of success, no matter what that definition is. If you are able to bolster your own EQ skills, you may find that you are far more likely to finally achieve that success when you reach for it.

Building Emotional Intelligence

Trying to figure out how best to build your emotional intelligence if you do not know what you are doing or where you are going is incredibly difficult. However, thanks to this book, you are getting a short guide right here. In fact, this section will provide you with several tips to help build your emotional intelligence to levels at which you will be far more effective in general.

Find Assertion

Remember, assertive is not the same as aggressive. If you can figure out how to be seen as assertive, you can ensure that people do not see you as too aggressive and, therefore, too threatening or too timid and therefore a risk of being abused into giving them free things, for example.

Learn active listening

It is critical for those who wish to be successful in having strong, active listening skills. When you find that your skillset, you commonly spend far too much time looking at yourself and how you feel instead of learning what other people are truly trying to communicate. For example, imagine that you are in a fight with your partner. If you are able to communicate clearly through the methods associated with emotional intelligence, you are far more likely to find that you are actually able to figure out the problem at the end of the day. Effectively, active listening will encourage attention and learning skills.

Developing your own motivation

One of the crucial differences between people who are successful and those who are not is primarily a matter of whether or not someone is able to put up with some negative behaviors and if you are willing to put up with it, but rather what your own motivations are. When you know what your own motivations are, you can usually figure out exactly what you need to do in order to actively and accurately what you want in life. Understanding your motivation and coming up with a goal for yourself can help immensely.

Become an optimist

Another critical skill in emotional intelligence is optimism. If you want to be optimistic, you are far more likely to succeed simply because you will have positive mindsets. Remember, mindsets are contagious, and if you think in a positive mindset, you are likely to attract more positivity to yourself as well. For this reason, you want to make it a point to always look on the bright side of things to ensure that you are actually as happy as you need to be in order to truly be successful in the first place.

Be self-aware

If you want to be successful, you must also be self-aware. In being self-aware, you are effectively able to self-regulate when you are not happy or optimistic. Effectively, you are able to begin progressing in your work because you no longer have to worry about actively trying to project something in particular. Your ability to become self-aware is all that you need.

Learn to Empathize

Success comes primarily from within you, but most of the time, other people are still relevant to it. You need to make sure that you interact with other people as well to be as successful as possible. This means then that you have no choice but to actively try to empathize with other people. Empathy brings with it better understanding, and better understanding brings with it better relationships, and those relationships push you in the right direction toward the success that you naturally want and crave.

Develop Open Body Language

Perhaps a critical skill, if you wish to be successful at anything involving other people, you are going to want to make sure that you actively develop body language that is inviting rather than shut off from the world. This means making it a priority to emphasize smiles, keeping your body language relaxed, and more. When you do this, you find that people are far friendlier than you realized. Effectively, people all want to see you and interact with you when you are actively friendly and helping other people out.

Developing Emotional Intelligence for Leadership

When you do actively decide that emotional intelligence is right for you or that you absolutely want to be in some sort of leadership position, perhaps the best thing that you can do is push those emotional intelligence skills in order to actually ensure that you are on the right track for leadership and success.

The Positivity Challenge

Considering that perhaps one of the largest threats to your success is your own attitude, especially if that attitude is one of indifference or negativity, changing your own mindset to become positive is one of the best ways to increase your chances of success. Consider for a moment how many negative thoughts go through your mind in the course of a day. You may find that you are happy one minute, but as soon as you drop a mug that shatters, you find yourself furious and telling yourself that you are stupid. This is problematic—you should never be that negative to yourself.

When you do find yourself in a negative moment, one of the best things that you can do is ensure that you are able to actively challenging negative thoughts with positive ones. You will be tasked with providing three positive tasks to anything you word one toward negatively.

For example, imagine that you tell yourself that you are stupid. Now, you must come up with three distinct positives, and they should all be about yourself. When you do this, you are effectively shifting your own thinking, allowing yourself to think in positive manners instead of the negative ones.

Effectively, you are actively teaching yourself to figure out how best to avoid all of the negativity by drowning it in a sea of positivity. Very quickly, after several reiterations of actively having to figure out how to positively address a situation that you have had a negative thought about, you are likely to begin sort of curtailing the habit, especially if it is tied to some sort of reward for yourself.

Gratefulness Challenge

Similar to the idea of having that positive thought challenge, you must also come up with a challenge about things that you are grateful for. You think, for example, that you are not grateful enough with what you got for Christmas because you feel like the items that were bought for you were items that probably would have been better served toward the other person. When you are attempting the gratefulness challenge, you effectively want to ensure that you are able to practice gratefulness on a regular basis. You want to make sure that you can actually recognize what you are happy to have that is not entitled to you, and you are happy to thank those who have worked so hard to give you what you have.

Perhaps one of the best ways to do a gratefulness challenge, however, is done on paper and pencil to write down what you are happy and grateful for. You may write down what you are grateful that you have food, for example, or that you are thankful for the clothing or dog food that was donated to a dog that had nothing to give. When you acknowledge out loud or on paper what you are grateful for, it can help you greatly in figuring out what to do next and where to go from there.

The Eye Contact Challenge

This does not mean that you should be actively attempting to have staring contests with everyone around you—instead, you should be actively attempting to maintain eye contact at a healthy level. You will want to be able to actively make that eye contact with other people if you ever hope to have a good chance of success. Because so much of success depends upon other people, you need to be able to look at people in the eyes.

If you are able to make eye contact, you are far more likely to be able to get that success simply because you will be better at interacting with other people. If you can do so, you will find that you are perceived to be better socially than if you were unable to make eye contact at all. To do this challenge, you must make it a point to work up to eye contact for extended periods of time with other people. In particular, the magic number is 50% when speaking, 70% of the time when listening. This is imperative—it is the perfect amount to let the other person know that you care about what they think while also actively avoiding staring down the other person to the point that he or she feels uncomfortable. Instead, you keep eye contact somewhat causal while still quite attentive with them.

Chapter 4: Body Language for Success

Imagine that you are standing in front of someone. You can see that they are crossing their arms with hands hidden behind them, their eyes shifting nervously from you to veer off to the left every now and then. They shift their weight from foot to foot and struggle to maintain eye contact. Something about the body language of this person makes you uneasy, but you cannot place it. They are keeping their distance from you, and every time you approach closer, you notice that they are likely to move away.

Body language is good at giving us feelings that tell us to be on edge, offended, or relaxed, but if you do not know what you are reading, you are going to struggle to understand why you are feeling that way. It can be difficult to know what someone intends if you cannot put meaning to what they are doing.
This chapter will take you through using body language to achieve your goals.

How to Control Your Body Language

Controlling your body language does not have to be difficult. If you are ready to begin controlling your body language once and for all, all you need to do is develop the ability to be self-aware and self-regulate. These skills are two foundational skills in emotional intelligence, but they do play a part in attempting to change your own body language as well. In developing this ability, you will start to see all of the benefits that you can gain from having good body language.

Confident Body Language

Finally, one last method that you can use to better your own communication with others is to develop confident body language. This means that you need to make sure that you do not close yourself off to contact other people. If you are quite conscientious about your body language, making sure that you portray yourself in a positive and attentive manner, you will find that you are actually far more effective in communicating with others.

This section will provide you with several different ways that you can keep your body language effective and confident in order to convince others to show confidence in you as well. If you can attract confidence, you will find that others are more receptive to your attempts to communicate with them.

- **Stand up tall:** The best way to be seen as assertive and confident is to keep your body language tall and open. The best way to do this is to straighten your spine, keep your head straight, and make sure that your legs are nicely spaced. You should stand with your feet at shoulder-width apart—doing so makes it clear to other people that you are confident and comfortable with yourself.

- **Use power poses:** Some poses, such as standing calmly and tall while your hands are behind your back, exude confidence without being overpowering. If you are able to use your power poses, you will not only tell other people that you are comfortable and confident, you will also begin to feel more confident as well.

- **Keep track of your hands:** Make sure you watch what your hands are doing. It can be incredibly easy to offend someone with a misplaced gesture or by hiding your hand in your pocket. Be mindful of what you do with them to ensure that you show that you are calm and in control.

- **Make good eye contact:** This cannot be more important or more emphasized—you need to be able to make good eye contact to be deemed as confident.

- **Avoid fidgeting:** People who are unconfident often find that they are regularly caught up in fidgeting or other nervous behaviors simply because they are uncomfortable. Their body betrays that lack of confidence. Try to stand still and open when you are communicating in order to be seen as confident.

- **Open body language:** Make sure that you keep your body language wide open. This means that you cannot be crossing your arms in front of you or otherwise attempting to hide when communicating. You want to ensure that the other person does not see you as dishonest or unwilling to communicate effectively.

Develop open body language

Perhaps a critical skill, if you wish to be successful at anything involving other people, you are going to want to make sure that you actively develop body language that is inviting rather than shut off from the world. This means making it a priority to emphasize smiles, keeping your body language relaxed, and more. When you do this, you find that people are far friendlier than you realized. Effectively, people all want to see you and interact with you when you are actively friendly and helping other people out.

Presenting yourself fairly for an interview

If you are going to an interview, you may be well aware that the nerves that come along with that initial drive and walk can be incredibly intimidating. Nevertheless, knowing how best to overcome, that means that you will be able to fight off the urge to run or do something else destructive. Instead, you can use your ability to read body language and to alter your own to help you make sure that you put your best foot forward and that you could respond to the actions of your interviewer effectively.

Chapter 5 Using Psychology to Fight Procrastination

And finally—you have arrived at the end of the book! Here, you will be tasked with figuring out exactly what you need to do, how to do it, and why it matters. Effectively, in this method, you will be figuring out exactly how you should approach situations of procrastination, which can be some of the most difficult to ever actually get out of simply due to the nature of the problem.

Everyone procrastinates now and then, however sometimes, it gets to a point in which it is overwhelming—it is so problematic that you are actively procrastinating that you fail to get things done by their deadlines much of the time. Slowly, bit by bit, you find that your procrastination is taking over your life and ruining it. You want to do your work, and you know that you have work to do, and yet instead, you find that you are stuck.

Within this last chapter, we will be addressing procrastination in general. We will look at what it is and what the problem with procrastination is. You will see some of the most common reasons people around you tend to procrastinate, and finally, you will be exposed to several of the methods through which you can defeat procrastination once and for all. In doing so, you may be surprised to find many of your issues relating to time management will disappear altogether.

In making these issues disappear, you may find that your stress level also declines dramatically, and with that decreased stress level, you may be better suited toward continuing to get your work done. This is good—with less procrastination comes more productivity, and that productivity is what you are looking for if you wish to be successful.

The Problem with Procrastination

Procrastination is incredibly difficult to cope with—it becomes habitual after a while, and it is only in demolishing that procrastination problem that you are ever actually able to defeat it. In defeating it, you will begin to improve your success, but until you get to that point, you are going to have to practice extreme self-control if you wish to bring that procrastination problem to a grinding halt.

First, let's look at what procrastination is. At its core, procrastination is the absence of doing what you should be at any given moment. You are actively choosing to do something contrary to what you should be, even though you know that you are making a bad choice. This means that it is nowhere near the same as laziness, which involves apathy. In this case, it is a willingness to do something entirely unrelated to what needs to get done.

Typically, people procrastinate because whatever it is that they have been tasked to do is boring, uncomfortable, or generally unpleasant in nature, and they decide that they are better off simply avoiding doing it altogether. However, all this does is cause more problems in the end. It leads to you instead trying to haphazardly rush through everything at the last minute instead of taking your time to get everything done with meticulous attention to detail as is usually expected of you.

Nevertheless, people everywhere continue to procrastinate. Even knowing that procrastination is something harmful, it is done anyway willingly. Of course, then, in response, work builds up instead of gets done. It becomes a matter of having a backlog of poorly done work instead of having your work done meticulously in advance, and that is problematic.

Why People Procrastinate

People tend to procrastinate for all sorts of reasons. Some do so because they are bored and do not want to do what they are supposed to be doing. Others do it because they would rather find something fun or enjoyable to do. Others still do it out of compulsive habit. They become so habituated to procrastination that it becomes this vicious cycle that is incredibly difficult to escape.

Consider for a moment that you have been procrastinating on that big paper for your politics class all week. You knew that it was coming up—it had been in your calendar for months, and yet, you still had not touched it. Knowing that it was due tomorrow, you looked it up this evening, only to find that you have no idea what you are doing. You choose to instead spend some time watching television instead of working on it.

A little bit later, you remind yourself that you have no choice but to get that work done if you want to actually get through it. You go to sit down at the paper, but you cannot help but feel stressed as you sit there. Soon, you are on social media instead of working, and soon after that, you find yourself constantly reading messages online.

Though you may not be aware of it, this is all because you have developed a tendency to be afraid of tests in general. You know that you usually struggle with tests, and because of that, you find that you stress out about them for a few weeks before they arrive. Of course, because you spend all of that time incredibly nervous and not studying effectively, you are nowhere near prepared on the morning of. You submit your paper and hope for the best.

In the end, you really struggled. However, that failure could actually have been a good thing. Had you been any quicker or they been any slower, you would have been able to figure out exactly how to tackle the problem sooner. However, instead, you failed and then took that failure to heart. That failure taken to heart becomes the reason that you struggle to get work done.

Effectively, getting the work done becomes stressful. When you are at work, you do not have any real leeway in your schedule. However, at home, that leeway is there—and you use it all and then some. This problem leads you to constantly be running late on everything.
However, if you were to stop and consider what was actually happening in the moment, you would realize that it was actually a cycle of anxiety.

You are afraid of failure, so you struggle to begin. In struggling to begin, you run late. In running late, you fail. You then effectively solidified that particular negative thought—you *did* fail. Therefore, you must be a failure.

Remaining stuck in that mindset is incredibly unproductive, however, and it is in your best interest to ensure that you are able to actively figure out how best to combat that as soon as you can.

The problem, however, is that the mind is effectively hardwired to follow the negative habit of procrastination. It is designed to avoid any sort of negativity. When you are procrastinating, you are avoiding some sort of negative stimulus, and at the end of the day, you are designed to do exactly that. Effectively, you get hit with anxiety, and that anxiety sends you into fight or flight mode. You then instinctively go into flight mode, allowing for further procrastination despite the fact that it is so incredibly harmful to the individual. You struggle to actually keep up, and your stress levels then skyrocket in response and you are left disappointing those counting on you.

Defeating Procrastination with Psychology

Defeating procrastination is all about learning how to kick back those feelings of negativity in order to bring back productivity. If you can get yourself working in productivity instead of negativity, you will find that you can begin to meet those deadlines once more. You can actively get yourself working toward exactly what you needed to since you will be motivated, rather than being avoidant.

While defeating your procrastination problem may seem incredibly intimidating, it is quite doable. At the end of the day, all you need to do is figure out how best to tap into your mind to visualize exactly what you want. You need to force your mind to see that procrastinating is the enemy—despite the fact that it seems to be exactly what you want in the moment, it is actually hurting you far more than it is helping, and that can be incredibly intimidating. When you feel like you cannot benefit from procrastination any longer, you may be more willing to avoid it in the future, essentially hijacking your mind to push toward motivation as the default state once more. As your mind accepts that motivated and achieving is the right state to be in, you will find that you are actually far more likely than ever to succeed. Your motivation is attractive to other people, and new opportunities will arise for you in the end. You will start to see long-term benefits that arise if you can just convince your mind that what you need to do more than anything else is to figure out how best to be motivated once more.

Visualize Your Future

Perhaps one of the most versatile tools that you have in your arsenal is your ability to visualize. You can visualize nearly anything—you can fantasize about something that you have always wanted, or you can fantasize about success. Ultimately, what you will be doing here is fantasizing over whatever it is that is incredibly important to you. If for you, what is important is success, you would envision that success exactly as you think it looks. Effectively, you want to show yourself exactly what it is that you want and exactly how you hope to get it. If you do this, you are likely to ensure that your mind gets a taste for what may be in store if you are able to actively push for it.

For example, imagine that you know that you have a vacation coming up. You know that you do not want to take your work on vacation, but you will have to do so if you do not take care of everything that needs to be done. Imagine for a moment how you would feel working away in your room while also watching out the window as people enjoy the beach outside without you. If you do not get that work done, that will be your future. You want to stress to yourself that in failing to meet that deadline for yourself, you are going to have no choice but to continue down that road. Remind yourself that you have plenty of time to actually meet your goals if you spend the time to get through all the work without actually procrastinating, and then encourage yourself to do exactly that. You want to make sure that you are able to actually get that work done so you can be free.

Now, imagine that same vacation if you were to spend the time to get your work done ahead of time. Think of the beach—the sand underneath your feet and the sound of the ocean lapping at the shore. Remind yourself that you would absolutely love to spend your time there instead of at home or in the hotel working. Remind yourself that the point of your vacation is to leave your work behind and to take a quick break. Tell yourself that if you want that break, you will need to work while committing that thought to memory. Burn the image of your vacation destination into your mind and summon it into your mind's eye every time you feel yourself beginning to procrastinate at all. In doing so, you will make sure that you deter yourself from procrastination every time you start to feel tempted to do so.

If done correctly, your mind will be willing to go through finishing the work as planned simply because it now feels like working on vacation is far worse than working at work when you'd rather watch another cat video. Because your mind is reminding itself that if you were to not work when it was work time, you would work more during the vacation, you will find that you are more likely to actively work and stay on schedule.

Accountability

People frequently find themselves workout buddies for the sole purpose of accountability. All things considered, working out with someone else can be quite distracting, but at the very least, it offers a level of accountability that you otherwise will not have. At that point, if you are to procrastinate, you will not only be letting yourself down—you will be letting down the other person as well. You will be making them go to the gym on their own instead of going with a friend that is going at the same time.

The idea of holding yourself accountable is incredibly powerful—humans tend to feel like they must be held accountable simply because telling other people that you have failed is generally not particularly enjoyable. If you have told other people that you were going to be doing something, you will feel the urge to ensure that you follow through simply due to the accountability.

Because people want to be seen as consistent, they tend to follow through when they voice that they are going to do something, and this is exactly why you end up doing exactly as promised when you are telling others what you are up to. Effectively, you are making sure that other people will follow up and ask you about your work, or you are making sure that someone else will be actively looking for you wherever you are supposed to be. If you are supposed to be at the gym working out, you will have someone looking for you and expecting you to spot them.

It is generally much harder for people to be willing to let down others than to let down themselves, and this is why it is so important to set up that accountability—people will follow along simply because they want to avoid letting down others who may be following or paying attention to what they are doing.

Bribes

Finally, one last way that you can keep yourself motivated is through the use of bribes. In psychology, this method is known as positive reinforcement—you actively reward good, positive behavior. Because of this, you can use bribes to effectively get people to stay on track with their work. You will do this if you want to ensure that everyone is doing what they said that they would do and what they need to do.

Imagine that you have a 30-page file to get through at work. You may feel like that is far too much and continue to push it off simply because you do not want to work on it. As you do this, you find that it is getting pushed off simply because you do not want to do it in the first place. With that in mind, you instead make it a point to actively bribe yourself to get through the work.

You decide that, after every 5 files you get through, you are free to spend 30 minutes playing a video game that you have been dying to play. Once all of the files are done, you tell yourself, you will buy yourself that new game that you have been dying to get your hands on as well. Effectively, you layer on so much positivity to what you need to get done that suddenly, getting through everything is a breeze. You may find that those files are finished up far quicker than they otherwise would have been, freeing you up and allowing you to move on with your life without worrying about procrastination continuing to eat away at your time and energy.

Eventually, you find that all files are done, and you feel quite accomplished and proud. This alone is a positive reinforcement, but when you add in the idea of actually getting a new game as well, you have doubly reinforced that new action. You are beginning to see procrastinating as less of an attempt to avoid work and more of an attempt to be lazy, and little by little, you find that you get better about actively finishing up all of your work without complaint. Eventually, you are even able to develop that internal motivation that comes from yourself. So long as you learn how to tap into that motivation, you will find that everything else comes naturally.

As with the vast majority of difficult tasks and difficult habits to break, the hardest part is the beginning. As soon as you get started and get past that first hurdle, it does get easier. It becomes easier and easier to find that intrinsic motivation within yourself to help you, and you are far more likely to succeed. All you need to do is get past that first push once and for all. Remember, you can do it. You just need to set your mind to it.

74

Chapter 6: Neuro-Linguistic Programming for a Successful Life

NLP is designed to help you facilitate getting the results that you want and need. It helps you figure out how best to act in ways that are conducive to your success. Those who practice NLP say that the unconscious mind is what drives you to achieve your goals, so long as you are able to communicate those goals effectively. NLP recognizes that both the conscious and unconscious minds are important and serve their own roles.

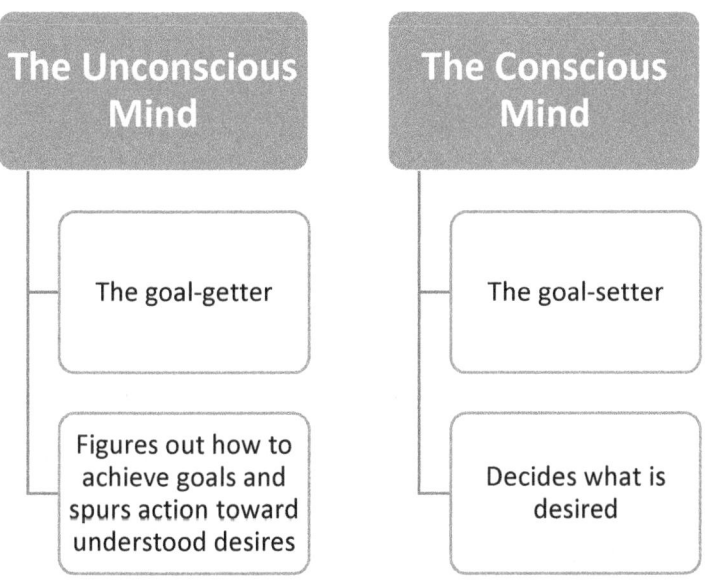

NLP helps to bridge that gap between the two, acting as a sort of translator, so your conscious desires are communicated to the unconscious mind in order to ensure that your mind works together rather than against each other. By working together, you will find that you are far more likely to see your desired results simply because you are not running into the problem of having the two parts of your mind clash.

Effectively, neuro-linguistic processing is a method of learning to communicate with the unconscious. You are learning to become fluent in your unconscious mind's method of communication so you can finally tell it what you want. It allows for that communication with yourself, but also facilitates the communication with others as well.

La storia della PNL

NLP, like nearly any psychological technique, has changed drastically from creation to what you now know and see today. While the root is still the same, there are different ways that the thoughts and techniques are approached now compared to what was seen back when it was first founded in the 1970s. This chapter will provide you with a brief overview of how NLP has changed and what you can expect if you were to use NLP today. Ultimately, you can think of NLP as what it was during creation and within the four waves of NLP.

The Creation of NLP

Created in 1972 by two psychotherapists named Richard Bandler and John Grinder, this process was originally designed to model several other therapeutic processes at the time. In particular, it referenced and developed from techniques such as gestalt therapy, hypnotherapy, and systemic family therapy. All of these came together to create an approach that would address two specific things: Why are psychotherapists special or skilled in influencing others? How can that specialty be transferred to other normal people without any formal training in psychology?

These two thoughts then triggered the beginning of the development of NLP. IN particular, people were taught to look at each of the aforementioned psychotherapy processes. Bandler and Grinder drew from those different forms of psychotherapy and pulled out any processes or techniques that they thought were critical in making the therapist so powerful. They identified the patters in communication and attitudes and were able to then create and build a list of techniques and beliefs drawing from those forms of psychotherapy. Thus, NLP was born.

NLP has primarily existed within four specific waves, during which different aspects were focused on or developed. These four waves are important to understand in order to truly understand what NLP was and what it has become.

- **Wave 1: NLPure:** In the first wave of NLP, you see the original NLP as developed by Bandler and Grinder. This is the purest form, during which success and enthusiasm were the most important factors that were pushed.

- **Wave 2: NLPt:** In the second wave, you see NLP used as an application in psychotherapy. It is commonly referred to as neuro-linguistic psychotherapy, and it began in 1989. This was all about making sure that people had a healthy and happy approach and view of life.

- **Wave 3: NLPeace:** This third wave, NLPeace, arose in 1992, with a focus on spirituality. Instead of focusing on how to fix the mind itself, it was focusing on how to find meaning in life and figure out how to connect spiritually.

- **Wave 4: NLPsy:** Finally, the fourth wave encompasses the use of neuro-linguistic processing as a form of psychology. Beginning in 2006, this was used to being to identify psychological patterns. It requires a master's degree in psychology, for a qualification to practice psychotherapy, and also an NLP master training qualification. Effectively, when you see someone that practices NLPsy, you know that they have gone through years of schooling in order to be as effective as possible when it comes to offering treatment.

When you seek out NLP treatment from a professional, you will likely face someone that is trained in fourth wave NLP. This is good—they are licensed to help you and can enable you to be the healthiest you that you can be. However, remember that NLP itself was designed to be accessible even to the average person. While you are not qualified to diagnose people if you have not gone to school to become licensed to do so, you will still be able to develop an affinity for several NLP processes so you can use them effectively and in ways that you know are beneficial to others around you or to yourself.

Conoscere il tuo risultato

The first and most important place to start when you are attempting to live with the utilization of NLP is knowing your outcome. This is effectively figuring out exactly what you want, how you will get it, and why you want it. If you do not know what the outcome you want is, how can you possibly hope to ever achieve it? If you do not know that you want to be a lawyer, for example, can you possibly reasonably expect yourself to go through law school and build up all that debt, only to find out after the fact that law was your passion after all? No—no one in their right mind would ever put themselves through law school without ever knowing that they wanted to be a lawyer or that their true goal in life was to be a lawyer. People may go through law school because they have been told their whole life that they should go to law school, but even those people grew up with the expectation of being a lawyer. No one goes to law school without the expectation or desire to become that person.

Just like no one would ever expect that you must know your own outcome and desires if you want to succeed. You need to figure out exactly what you want in life so you can figure out how to get it. Do you want to be rich? Do you want to find love? Maybe you want to be a parent, or you want to become a firefighter. No matter what the dream is, you need to know and vocalize it to yourself if you want it to become a reality. If you want to be rich, you can tell yourself that. If you want to be happy, you can tell yourself that, too. What your goal is in life is not as important as knowing what that goal is. That knowledge is power and will help you during your process.

If you are using NLP for other people, you may want to know what your end goal for that person is. Do you want them to be happy? Do you want them to buy that car you are selling? Maybe you want them to break up with their narcissistic partner. No matter what it is you want, you need to know what it is if you hope to make it happen.

Once you know what you want, it is time to form it in a way that you can act upon it. This is effectively just coming up with a way to structure your desires so you can act upon them. When you do this, you must meet certain specific criteria to ensure that the outcome is well-formed. This is a fancy way of saying that if you want your goal to be actionable and attainable, you need to word it in the proper manner. These criteria are critical to making sure that you are able to act accordingly. These criteria are:

- **Positive-oriented:** Your goal must be focused on what you *do* want, not what you would like to avoid. For example, you must state that you want to find love, versus you don't want to be alone any longer. Shifting this to a positive instead of a negative gives you something to work toward instead of something to avoid.

- **Sensory specific:** As we continue along the NLP path, you will begin to see that every method of influence on someone else, whether it is on yourself or on someone else, is sensory. You must figure out which senses you will be targeting and how those senses will perceive when you have been successful at achieving your goal. Perhaps this will be that you can see that you have a partner if your end goal is to find love. If you want to sell that car, perhaps you decide that the sensory input will be having the paperwork with the signatures in your hand. Try to address how each of your five senses will interact with the outcome when it has been achieved. This helps you be able to truly visualize what you want.

- **Contextual:** This involves making sure that you know the context under which you will be successful. You are acknowledging what has to happen if you want to be successful. Where will it happen? When? How? Who will you be with? When you know the context of what you are seeking, you will be able to acknowledge what you need to do to set up the environment properly to ensure that you do happen to get whatever you are hoping to achieve.

- **Self-achievable:** You must make sure that the goal you want is one that you can set into action on your own without the influence of other people. You may need to make sure that other people are doing something, but can you do so? You must have access to the resources that you will need to achieve your goal.

- **Ecological:** This is as simple as asking three specific questions for yourself: Is it good for you? Is it good for other people? Is it for the greater good? Remember, NLP is all about bettering the world and those who are using it. While it is often used as a tool for manipulation and controlling others, that is not always the intention.

- **Worthwhile:** Finally, you must make sure that whatever the outcome that you are trying to achieve is worthwhile. Is it something that will actually be useful and positive to you? It does not have to be useful on a daily basis, but you should be able to see some good from whatever it is. You may have enhanced other people's lives, allowing your friend to no longer be terrified of crowds, which indirectly improves your own life because your friend is happier and healthier. On the other hand, you may directly address a problem of your own in an attempt to better yourself, and that is okay too. So long as it is effective, either directly or indirectly, it is good enough.

Take action

The next step to making sure that you are able to be successful in using NLP is to take action. This is something that may seem like common sense, but many people entirely miss this step altogether. You must be willing to act if you hope to see any results. If you want to ensure that you can actually change your life or change the behaviors of someone else, you must figure out reasons to work or do something.

Oftentimes, people fall into the trap of inaction—they feel like they cannot possibly succeed, and therefore they fall victim to procrastination. However, this is your mind's attempt to avoid action in order to protect yourself from failure. When you protect yourself in this way, it is easy to make excuses and act like it happened for a reason- you may tell yourself that you are too dumb to really make a difference, or that you will fail even if you try.

Well, guess what: Failure happens. People fail all the time, but that is not inherently bad. When you fail, you learn. When you learn, you become better prepared for your next attempt. It is okay to fail, so long as you learn from that failure and do not let it define you. Effectively, then, you want to live through learning from that failure and not letting the fear of failure keep you locked in inaction.

When you are practicing NLP, you *must* act. If you refuse to act, nothing gets done. Nothing changes. People's behaviors remain the same. You fail. NLP is not passive—it requires constant action and effort, and for that reason, you must be willing to go through the motions and make whatever it is that you want happen.

Do you have some sort of negative trauma that makes it difficult for you to function? Perhaps you feel like you have been held back by your emotions or attempts to get through life. Well, after reading this book, you now have several tools that can help you feel better about who you are, what you want, and how you live life. All you need to do is begin to utilize them.

NLP can be used upon yourself regularly enough to make yourself happier, healthier, and more confident. In attracting happiness and confidence, you will find that you are far more successful in your endeavors. You may realize that you are able to better communicate and relate to people after having defeated your anxiety or fears. You may find that you are able to get along better because you can communicate easier. You may find that you are simply feeling better without that concern over how people will see you is gone.

When you are able to wield NLP for yourself, you can begin to defeat any traumas that have lingered, holding you back for far too long. You will be able to reframe those traumas, separating from that negativity and figuring out ways to make those memories something far less traumatic. You will be able to anchor yourself in a process that is incredibly similar to the one used for other people, and with using this, you will find that you are able to defeat negative habits. With those habits gone, you will feel far more capable. You will be empowered. You will be successful. You will be using NLP for its truest purpose—to wield to help others and yourself.

This chapter will guide you through three techniques that you can use to wield the power of NLP on yourself. You will learn how to use dissociation in order to distance yourself from feelings related to a specific traumatic event or to remove a trigger between an event and a feeling. You will learn to use reframing to change the way that you view an event or memory. Lastly, you will be guided through how to anchor yourself with ease.

Chapter 7: The Importance of Empathy for Achieving Success

Empathy is one of those buzzwords that you hear thrown around a lot in modern psychology and self-help sources. You may hear the empath discussed, especially in regards to narcissism. You may hear people say that they are an empath at heart, or that they are incredibly empathetic. However, do you know what is meant by calling someone an empath?

Empaths are people who are highly in tune to their surroundings and those within them. In particular, they are usually able to sense the feelings of others with ease. This is a skill known as empathy, and this is a critical skill for people to master. Empathy is the skill that the narcissist does not have— he cannot empathize, and because he cannot empathize, he cannot effectively manage to relate to other people.

How about you? Are you empathetic? Do you have a good idea of what empathy is? Do you want to be more empathetic? What can empathetic behavior help you do, and how can it be beneficial?

All of these are fantastic questions to ask if you are unfamiliar with the concept of empathy itself. Even if you are unfamiliar, do not fret—this chapter is focused on empathy and how you can use it to protect yourself. In particular, we will delve into looking at what empathy is, what the types of empathy are, and how empathy can be used to help you better yourself. You will see how empathy can fight narcissism, as well as how you can use it to become less susceptible to narcissism as a whole.

What is Empathy?

Empathy, at its simplest, is the human capacity to relate to other people. You use empathy to help facilitate communication, for example, in order to better understand those around you. It allows you to understand what those around you are feeling in particular, allowing you to essentially step into the shoes of the other person by relating to them.

Imagine for a moment that you are walking down the street and you see a homeless person sitting out in the rain. You feel sad for the person because he is stuck out in the rain and it is cold. You understand what it means to be cold and wet, something that you have been before, though maybe not within the same context, and you feel empathetic for the man. You know that he is likely suffering, and that makes you feel sad and hopeless. Effectively, you take on the feelings of the other person in order to relate to him. Empathy then has two very serious functions: Communication and regulation

When you are able to communicate your emotional state to other people, you are effectively able to make sure that you are actively broadcasting out your needs. After all, emotions are closely linked to needs that must be met, so when you are having your emotions read by someone else, they are effectively learning what your needs are. If they see that you are sad, they are likely to know that you need support, simply because that is what sadness conveys—a need for support. If they see that you are afraid, they are going to know that what you need is safety, as something present around you is frightening you.

Empathy then allows for nonverbal communication. It allows for people to tell others exactly what they need at that given moment without them having to ever say a word. Think of how effective that is—how long would it take if every time that you had a feeling, you had to verbally express that you were happy or sad? You would spend an awful long time talking about your constantly fluctuating emotions, especially since emotions are not particularly stable in the first place. Emotions are constantly fluctuating; sometimes, every few seconds, and empathy allows for their communication easily.

Empathy to Increase Self-Awareness

Beyond just to understand people, empathy is actually quite useful in the development of other social skills as well. In particular, empathy is a great segue to self-awareness, and that self-awareness can really help you to fight off the tendency to fall into aggressive or abusive relationships. When you are self-aware, you recognize yourself. You know what your true abilities and feelings are, and that your self-awareness is accurate. In particular, self-awareness is necessary if you want to be able to regulate your own behaviors, thanks to knowing your limits.

When you are not particularly self-aware, you run into a lot of the same problems that the narcissist suffers from. You will find that you cannot regulate yourself effectively, and if you cannot understand your own feelings, you are not going to be able to understand the feelings of others, either.

However, if you already have a base of being highly empathetic, you can try to use that empathy to really help you understand other people as well. If you can see what someone else's body, language is saying.

Ultimately, your self-awareness and ability to empathize are far closer related than you may have thought, and the more empathy you have, the more likely you are to make it a point to regulate what you are saying. That regulation of understanding what is going on is what will help you with the development of self-awareness. If you know that your actions are upsetting other people, for example, you are coming across in a way that is clearly inappropriate in the eyes of other people. This means that other people are entirely unhappy with how you are presenting yourself, and you will need to figure out why.

Your empathy then allows you to start figuring out why they were unhappy. What did you do that caused it? If you see that in particular, people seem to be annoyed with your insistence to do something a certain way, you could assume that your desire to complete whatever it was is the problem. Perhaps you were coming across as pushy.

Now, you are able to acknowledge that the people were annoyed with you, and then figure out exactly why. When you are aware of what you are doing and how it is impacting those around you, you are far more likely to be cautious in the future. You will then be more self-aware.

Effectively, then, self-awareness is regulated by empathy, and that makes the two quite powerful when used in tandem.

Empathy to Build Self-Esteem

Just as empathy and self-awareness are closely related, you must also be able to acknowledge the fact that empathy and self-esteem share a similar bond. Self-esteem is critical to how we see ourselves. Your own self-esteem is largely the way that you view yourself in the world. Are you happy with who you are, or do you feel like something about your personality is inherently flawed? Do you feel like your ability to help other people is so incredibly stunted that you are not particularly valuable, or do you think that you are a good person?

Think about self-esteem for a moment and what the words may mean. You are literally creating an estimate of yourself. You are effectively defining your value, as seen in your own eyes. If you have a high self-esteem, or a healthy self-esteem, you view yourself quite positively. Some people's self-esteem may be too high, such as the narcissist—but in moderation, self-esteem is critical to being successful in the world around you. If you have a healthy self-esteem, you have your own boundaries and limits for yourself. You are effectively able to say that you respect yourself and put a line on where that respect is. You can tell what you think about yourself by looking at that line.

Low self-esteem, however, implies that your image of yourself is quite negative. You feel like the image that you present is problematic or flawed, or you feel like the person that you are is inherently negative. When you have a low self-esteem, you do not trust yourself. You do not think that the person that you are is worthy of respect or love, or you may even feel like you are a waste of space and time in the world.

Self-esteem is one of those traits that you want in moderation in order to be healthy, and empathy can help you achieve exactly that. Consider, for a moment, the effect of mutual empathy.

For example, imagine that you and your friend are able to empathize with each other. You are able to respect each other and show each other how much you care about each other. You can make sure that you are able to show the other person your own assessment of their own worth. You value them, and you are able to show that through relating to their feelings. The more you empathize with someone, the more you value who they are, what they like, and how you see them.

Now, if you just empathized with your friend, how do you think that made him feel?

The answer is that he probably felt pretty good—he was justified by you acknowledging his position and his own feelings, and that was something that he truly appreciated. You effectively showed him that he cared, and in response, he was happier than he had been in a while.

Now, consider that the empathy is mutual—he empathized with you when you were talking about the problem with the narcissist that you have recently escaped from. You feel validated and supported, as well.

When you feel like people validate and support you, you feel like other people are hearing who you are and actually caring about what you are saying. This means that you are able to see that other people are, in fact, acknowledging you, your feelings, and your likes and dislikes. You are seeing that, unlike how the narcissist told you, you do have inherent value. The narcissist may have damaged your self-esteem by refusing to acknowledge your values and emotions, but you can begin to heal from that.

You can draw from the empathy of others to begin to heal those wounds.

Empathy reminds you that others in the world do, in fact, care about you. They do care what you think about the world. They do care how you are feeling and whether you can claim that all of your needs have been met. They want to ensure that you are able to take care of yourself, and they are able to help.

If even random strangers that you do not know can empathize with you, then what does that tell you? It tells you that your self-esteem should improve. It tells you that your narcissistic ex's attempts to belittle you and bring you down were little more than tools to keep you easily subdued, and without the narcissist present, you should be willing to acknowledge this.

This means then that without the narcissist to continue bringing you down you should be able to begin healing more and more. You can make sure that you are actually beginning to feel better, and acknowledging that you do have an inherent value that other people see. Empathy will remind you to heal that inherent value. It will help that damaged; wilted self-esteem begin to blossom and flourish once more, nourished upon the love and empathy from other people. If other people can see your value without knowing you, then you must have some.

Conclusion

Congratulations! You have reached the end of ***The Psychology of Success.***

We hope this has been an incredibly informative process for you. As always, with psychology topics, it can be difficult to find a book and topic that is truly interesting and also easy to understand, but we hope that you found this book to be interesting, easily understandable, useful, and actionable.

Throughout this book, you were given advice that was meant to be actionable. Whenever possible, you were given step-by-step guidance, and hopefully you found it helpful as you prepare to take these tips into the real world.

You were guided on how to use body language to show a confident appearance, how to use NLP to achieve your goals, how to increase self-awareness with empathy, and how to use psychology to combat procrastination.

Of course, there's still a lot to learn; you're not an expert yet. From here, you could delve even deeper.
Several concepts are briefly introduced in this book, such as neuro-linguistic programming or empathy.

After all, the topics discussed in this book had one purpose: have a successful life!

Thank you so much for allowing me to join you on this journey. While this book is coming to a close, the rest of your journey is not. There are several other books that relate to this one, if you found it particularly helpful or compelling.

CPSIA information can be obtained
at www.ICGtesting.com
Printed in the USA
BVHW082028100521
606946BV00006B/1359